BULLETPOINTS

HORSE CARE

Marion Curry

Miles Kelly
PUBLISHING

First published in 2005 by Miles Kelly Publishing Ltd
Bardfield Centre, Great Bardfield
Essex, CM7 4SL

Editorial Director: Belinda Gallagher
Editorial Assistant: Hannah Todd **Designer:** Neil Sargent, DPI Colour
Picture Research: Liberty Newton **Production:** Estela Boulton

British Library Cataloguing-in-Publication Data
A catalogue record for this book is available from the British Library

ISBN 1-84236-530-4

Printed in China

www.mileskelly.net
info@mileskelly.net

The publishers would like to thank the following artists who have contributed to this book:
Steve Caldwell (Allied Artists), Jim Channel, Terry Gabbey, Sally Holmes, Richard Hook (Linden Artists), Janos Marffy,
Angus McBride, Andrea M⸻e (Temple Rogers)

The publishers would ⸻ photographs:
Pages 4, 11, 31, Lisa Clayden; ⸻ b Langrish; 16, 17, 19,
E Jeffries and Sons Ltd; 1⸻ ⸻hart Stables Ltd

All o⸻

Contents

The healthy horse

▲ *A healthy horse's general appearance is one of well-being. It will appear relaxed and content in the paddock.*

- **When looking after a horse**, it is important to be aware of what is 'normal' for the individual. If a horse is behaving unusually, its carer is quickly aware of the situation and can act promptly.

- **A healthy horse** has bright clear eyes, which are not weeping or discharging down its nose. The ears should be alert, not drooping or uninterested or held tightly back.

- **The normal temperature** of a horse is 37.5 to 38.5°C (99.5 to 101.3°F).

- **Respiration at rest** should be between 10 to 20 inhalations a minute.

- **A horse's pulse** rate is normally 35 to 45 heart beats a minute at rest.

- **The coat** should be supple and shiny, not dull and staring.

▶ *Much can be surmized about a horse's health simply by taking a good look at its demeanour and expression. A interested expression suggests the horse is not unwell or in distress.*

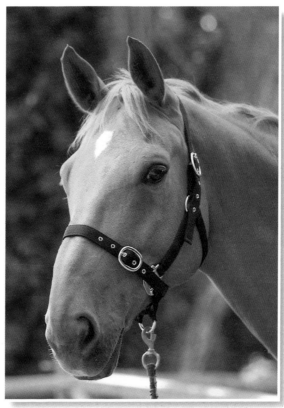

- **A healthy horse supports** its weight on all four feet equally and shows no sign of swelling or heat in its feet or legs.

- **The sounds** coming from a horse's stomach should be 'normal' for that individual and not particularly loud. The stomach should not be distended and the horse should be eating and drinking normally.

- **The tail** should be relaxed and not clamped down between the horse's back legs.

- **A horse should not stand** in a depressed manner at the back of its stable or away from companions in the paddock. Any signs of irritable or untypical behaviour may indicate the horse is feeling unwell.

Points and condition

- **A horse's body parts** are identified through a series of points. These recognized terms are used to pinpoint particular areas of the body.

- **Condition** refers to a horse's outward appearance of health. A shiny coat, clear eyes, clean nose and ribs that can be felt but not seen, are all indicators of good condition.

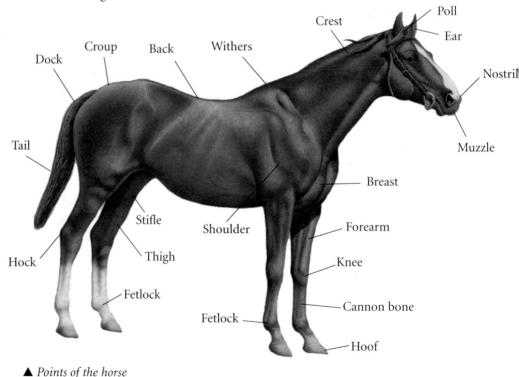

▲ *Points of the horse*

- **Worms that live** in a horse's system are parasites. If left undisturbed, they result in loss of condition and in cases of severe infestation, colic.

- **Regular worming** throughout the year is essential in domestic horses to keep infestation under control.

- **Laminitis is** a painful foot condition which restricts the blood flow to the feet. An affected horse will often stand, placing its weight on its heels, to relieve the pain.

- **A horse's temperament** cannot be quickly assessed. It is necessary to study a horse's behaviour in relation to other horses, as well as its interaction with humans. This determines whether it is generally a quiet, dependable sort or an independent flighty animal.

- **Hocks are joints** on a horse's hind legs.

- **The withers should** be the highest point on a horse's back. They are found at the base of the mane.

- **Heels are found** on the underside of a horse's foot. A farrier must take care when shoeing that the shoe does not impinge on the heel, causing corns.

- **Fetlock joints** are found on all four legs. They are below the horse's knee on its front legs and below the hocks on its back legs.

Feet

- **Horses are odd-toed** animals, having only one toe or hoof on each leg.

- **In the wild**, horses wear their feet down naturally. Domestic horses, however, usually need to have their feet trimmed about every six weeks.

- **Horses that work** or travel on hard roads need their hooves protected by metal shoes. These need to be replaced every 4 to 6 weeks.

- **The person who** cares for a horse's feet is called a farrier.

- **To measure a horse** or pony's foot for shoes, take the measurement across the widest part of the foot and also from the toe to the heel. Front and hind feet may be different sizes.

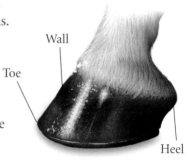

Wall

Toe

Heel

- **Hooves are made** of keratin, a protein that is the same substance as hair or human nails.

- **The frog** is the rubbery wedge-shaped part on the underside of a horse's hoof. It helps absorb shock as its hoof hits the ground, and prevents slipping.

- **Mud can absorb** moisture from the hoof wall and make it brittle.

- **A horse often paws** the ground with a front foot prior to rolling. Pawing can also be a sign of frustration.

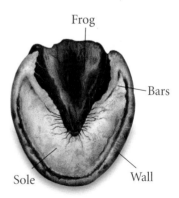

Frog

Bars

Sole

Wall

▲ *The outside layer of the hoof is insensitive and allows for shoes to be nailed on.*

····· ···· ···· ···· ···· ···· ···· ···· ···· ····

> ···FASCINATING FACT···
> Horseshoes are considered lucky and replicas are
> often carried by brides on their wedding day.

Traditional front horseshoe

Traditional hind horseshoe

Remedial shoes to help alleviate foot problems

Lightweight racing plate

▲ *Different styles of horseshoe can be fitted. The shape and materials are chosen to suit the needs of the horse.*

Feeds and feeding

- **Horses have small stomachs** for their size and need to eat little and often. If kept in a field, horses will graze for most of the day. If forage is insufficient to meet the nutritional requirements of the horse, particularly those in work, additional feed may be needed.

- **Feed is one of the main costs** of keeping horses. However, feeding horses well-balanced diets is also the principal way of keeping horses healthy.

- **When choosing** a suitable diet for a horse, there are many of different feedstuffs: concentrates, forage, supplements, vitamins, and herbs. However, grass is the most natural foodstuff and roughage must play the largest part in their diet.

- **Bought foodstuffs** fall into two basic categories: forage, such as hay and haylage, and concentrates, such as cereals, mixes, nuts and pellets.

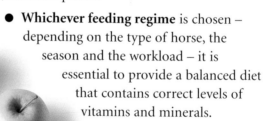

- **Whichever feeding regime** is chosen – depending on the type of horse, the season and the workload – it is essential to provide a balanced diet that contains correct levels of vitamins and minerals.

◀ *Succulents, such as apples and carrots, can be added to a feed ration to make it more appetizing.*

- **Proprietary balanced feeds** offer a consistent diet and are convenient to use. They are carefully formulated to meet the requirements of different types of horses and workloads, from high-fibre maintenance to high-energy performance rations.

- **All concentrates** should be kept in rodent-proof containers to avoid attracting vermin and wasting food. Hay should be stored off the ground in a dry, ventilated area.

- **Before purchase**, hay should be inspected to guarantee it is free from ragwort. It should not appear dusty, smell bad or have any visible mould.

- **Sudden changes** in the type of food can cause digestive upset. All changes to the diet should be undertaken on a gradual basis.

- **Clean water** must be available at all times – either from a self-filling container or from a trough. In winter, water containers should be provided in frost-free areas to ensure the horse has a ready supply of water during cold weather.

Grooming kit

- **Every domestic horse** should have its own grooming kit that is kept solely for its own use. This prevents infectious skin conditions being passed to other animals. The kit keeps the horse clean and healthy and its feet free from stones.

- **The basic kit** consists of brushes, sponges, a hoof pick and a means of cleaning the brushes. It is important to regularly remove dirt, hair and old skin matter.

- **The dandy brush** is used to remove dried mud and dirt from a horse's winter coat. It has long, stiff bristles and is usually used on the less sensitive parts of the horse's body.

- **The body brush** is softer and is used to remove grease and dust from a horse's summer coat. It can be used on sensitive areas such as the head, stomach, or inside the legs.

- **A water brush** is used for applying water to the horse's coat, mane and tail when dampening or washing.

- **A rubber or plastic curry comb** is used to remove dried mud and loose hair from the coat. A metal curry comb should never be used on a horse but is used to remove dust and dirt from the brushes.

- **Mane combs** are often metal, but sometimes plastic, and are used to comb the mane and tail of the horse.

- **Hoof picks** are used for removing dirt and stones packed into the underside of a horse's hoof. Hooves should be picked out daily.

- **Stable sponges** are ordinary foam sponges used for cleaning the eyes, nose, nuzzle and tail area. A stable rubber or good linen drying-up cloth can be dampened and gently wiped over the body to give the horse a final polish.

- **Where horseowners share** facilities, for example at a livery yard, each brush should be labelled with the owner's or horse's name. Grooming should be done outside so that dust is not inhaled. A lightweight plastic container or a canvas bag with drawstring top makes an excellent storage for a grooming kit.

▲ *An everyday grooming kit should contain items essential for keeping a horse clean.*

Grooming

- **A carer should be properly dressed** for dealing with horses, wearing gloves, stout boots and, if necessary, a riding hat.

- **A headcollar and leading rope** should be put on the horse before bringing it out of its stable or field.

- **The horse should be tied up** using a slip knot that can be easily undone if necessary. Any rugs should be removed. If it is very cold, rugs can be turned over on themselves, leaving only a part of the horse's body exposed. This is known as quartering.

- **Grooming should begin** with picking out the feet. Mud, stones and dirt should be removed so that the horse does not pick them up in its hooves again.

Dandy brush

- **The next stage** is to remove any mud or dirt from the horse's coat. In winter, a rubber curry comb and dandy brush will remove dried mud, but if the horse is kept outdoors, care should be taken not to overgroom, as natural grease in a horse's coat helps to keep it warm and dry.

Body brush

▲ *Different types of grooming brush can be used during a grooming session. Grooming stimulates circulation and helps keep the coat and skin clean and healthy.*

● **During summer**, on clipped horses or on sensitive areas of the body, a soft body brush should be used. The face should cleaned using a soft brush and sponge. It is best to untie the horse while cleaning this area, holding onto the leading rope with one hand.

● **Particular care** should be taken to thoroughly groom the areas where tack sits.

● **Brushes should be cleaned** repeatedly against a metal curry comb during the course of grooming.

● **A thorough grooming**, massaging the skin, removes dirt from the coat and makes the horse look clean and shiny. Once the neck and body are finished, including the legs, the mane and tail should be carefully brushed out.

● **While grooming** never sit or kneel down next to the horse. Always squat, in case the horse is startled and moves suddenly.

▶ *A horse or pony should be happy to be touched all over, and should stand still, without fidgeting, while being groomed.*

15

Saddles

- **Saddles are a vital piece** of equestrian equipment. A good well-fitting saddle carries the rider in the correct position without causing the horse any discomfort.

- **Traditionally made** from leather, lighter synthetic saddles are now popular. They come in a variety of seat sizes to suit the rider and a number of different styles, such as pony, jumping, dressage and general-purpose.

- **Saddles should be cleaned** and checked regularly to ensure the stitching is safe and there are no lumps forming underneath the seat that could damage the horse's back.

- **When buying a new saddle**, an experienced saddle fitter should fit one which is appropriate for both horse and rider.

- **As horses change shape** through losing or gaining fitness, the fit of a saddle should be reassessed regularly.

- **Numnahs are saddle-shaped** pads that sit underneath the saddle to protect the horse's back and should not be used to try to correct an ill-fitting saddle. They also help keep the saddle free from dirt and sweat.

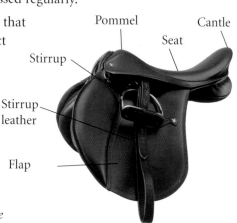

Pommel · Seat · Cantle · Stirrup · Stirrup leather · Flap

▶ *To ensure saddles are safe for use, the stitching, girth straps and leathers should be regularly checked for wear and cracks.*

- **Girths secure a saddle** on the horse and come in a variety of shapes, materials and designs, depending on the discipline. They must not rub the horse or damage the delicate skin around its middle.

◀ A dressage saddle has a straighter cut and is slimmer fitting than a general-purpose saddle. This allows the rider a closer connection to the horse and an elongated leg position.

- **Stirrup leathers** are the two leather loops suspended from a saddle that hold the metal foot rest – the stirrups – to support the rider's feet. Although traditionally referred to as 'leathers', they are now also available in webbing and synthetic material.

- **Stirrup irons** should be big enough to allow about 1 cm (0.5 in) of clearance each side of the rider's boot.

. . . . **FASCINATING FACT** . . . .
The *Selle Royale* saddle was developed in the 17th century. This saddle is still used by the Cadre Noir in France today.

Bridles

- **A bridle is headgear** used to control a horse's movement and direction and is a rider's primary means of communication with its head, mouth and nose.

- **Like saddles**, most bridles are made of leather but now also come in different materials such as webbing which has the advantage of being easily cleaned.

- **Bridles come** in three basic sizes: pony, cob and full size. The pieces can be mixed and matched to suit each animal. They can be adjusted easily to ensure a good fit, and taken apart for cleaning.

- **A snaffle bridle** consists of several pieces that fit together: a headpiece, a throatlash, two cheek pieces, a brow band, a nose band, a pair of reins and a snaffle bit.

▶ *The simplest form of English-style bridle is called a snaffle bridle.*

- **A bit is part** of a bridle that fits into a horse's mouth. Different styles of bit include the snaffle, the curb and the Pelham.

- **Bits are made** in different materials, including metal and rubber, and in various sizes.

- **A correctly sized bit** should show 0.5 cm (0.25 in) either side of the horse's mouth to ensure it does not pinch its lips.

- **Some bridles are bitless**, such as the hackamore, and work by adding pressure on a horse's nose.

- **Whichever bridle is chosen**, it is important to keep it clean by regularly removing dirt and sweat, and cleaning the bit in running water after use. Well-maintained saddlery is vital for the comfort and safety of horse and rider and will help to ensure that the tack lasts.

- **Where a horse has** a particularly thick mane, it is common to remove a 2 cm (1 in) strip of mane to allow the bridle headpiece to fit tidily behind its ears.

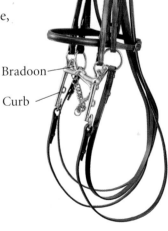

Bradoon

Curb

▶ *A double bridle has two metal bits – a bradoon (snaffle bit) and a curb bit, and two sets of reins. This type of bridle is used for showing and dressage and should only be used by experienced riders.*

Tacking up

- **A horse should be clean** prior to being tacked up. It should be approached in a calm manner. The bridle should be secured over one shoulder and the saddle carried over one arm with the girth looped over it. The stirrups should be positioned at the top of the stirrup leathers.

- **The underside of the saddle** should be checked by running a hand over it, and any numnah or saddlecloth, to ensure there are no sharp objects or insects.

▼ *The rider should stand close to the horse while tacking up, using calm unhurried movements. Time should be taken to check that there are no twisted straps and that the numnah or saddle cloth is not creased or folded over.*

- **The rider should stand** on the horse's left-hand side. The saddle should be positioned on top of the numnah and slid back into the correct place. The numnah should be drawn well up into the gullet of the saddle to ensure that it does not press down onto the horse's withers.

- **The saddle should sit** far enough back to allow free movement of the horse's shoulders.

- **The rider should walk** around the front of the horse to drop the girth down from the saddle, then return to the left-hand side to fasten the girth so that the saddle is secure.

- **To put on the bridle**, the rider should stand to the horse's left alongside its head. The reins are then passed over the horse's head.

- **The bit is introduced** to the horse's mouth by inserting a thumb into the gap in its teeth, which helps to open the mouth and place the nose through the noseband.

- **The headpiece** is then fitted over the ears, the throatlash fastened and the noseband done up. Finally, a check should be made that no pieces of the bridle have been tangled and that the horse's forelock is lying tidily over the browband.

- **The rider** should then recheck the girth and tighten if necessary. The girth buckle guards should be pulled down and the horse's front legs stretched forward to ensure that there is no skin trapped beneath the girth.

- **Horses should not be left** tacked up for any length of time as they might try to roll, injuring their backs and possibly breaking the saddle.

Rider wear

- **Someone riding** for the first time at a riding school need very little equipment. Clothing should not be too tight or uncomfortable and possession of a pair of stout boots with a small heel is all that is necessary. Most riding schools are happy to provide safety hats for beginners.

- **Riding clothes are designed** to be practical and smart, but above all to give the rider protection in the event of an accident. A rider should always wear a protective hat that meets current safety standards.

- **Jodphurs or breeches** are comfortable and practical and protect the legs from being pinched or chaffed from stirrup leathers.

- **A body protector** provides protection for the back, neck and shoulders, and is a good investment.

▶ *Long or short boots can be worn for general riding.*

▶ *An approved safety hat should always be worn for horseriding.*
A velvet-covered hat should be worn for competition riding.

- **Short or full-length leather boots** with a clearly defined heel give ankle support and prevent a rider's foot slipping through the stirrup. Wellington boots, while ideal for working in the paddock, should not be worn for riding as they may get caught in the stirrups.

- **A comfortable sweatshirt** or jumper and a warm jacket or waterproof coat are needed for riding outdoors. Fluorescent vests, called tabards, worn over outerwear help make riders more visible to road users.

- **Gloves are essential**, both to keep hands warm and to prevent the reins being pulled out of a rider's hands.

- **Long hair** should be neatly tied back.

- **Earrings** or any other form of jewellery should be removed before riding.

- **Riders wishing to take part** in competitive riding, such as showing, jumping or cross-country, will find there are dress codes for each discipline which must be adhered to.

Learning to ride

- **In Britain** there are over 700 British Horse Society approved riding schools.

- **Riding schools should be** checked out by visiting them rather than simply booking a lesson by telephone. This enables a new customer to determine how the animals look, the condition of the stables and fields, and the facilities the school has to offer, for example indoor and outdoor arenas, floodlit areas, cross-country jumps and hacking.

- **Beginners can expect** to be provided with riding hats. They will be introduced to a suitably sized, calm mount and shown how to get onto the horse.

- **The first lesson** will probably be conducted on a leading rein with a competent adult walking alongside the horse.

- **The rider will be taught** how to approach a horse correctly, how to mount and dismount, sit correctly and how to hold the reins.

- **A new rider will master** the basics of balance and stability in the saddle, so that they do not injure the horse's mouth or back.

- **Children will gain confidence** as the riding instructor introduces fun movements into the sessions. They will be expected to take their feet out of the stirrups and 'go around the world' on their ponies, turning to face the pony's tail and side, or lie back on their pony's back to touch its tail.

- **Rising trot** will be taught so that the rider feels the movement of the horse underneath and learns to 'post' or rise in time with the stride.

- **Canter should be introduced** later when the rider has a confident seat and is able to control the speed and direction of the horse.

- **Jumping is taught** when the rider is proficient at all the basics of controlling speed, turning and stopping and has a good balanced seat and hands that do not interfere with the horse's mouth.

▶ *Private one-to-one lessons are sometimes preferred by adults, but children usually enjoy the company and competitiveness of others.*

25

Road safety

- **When riding on roads** safety issues are very important for both horse, rider and other road users.

- **If possible riders should always travel** with another rider, or a friend on a bicycle or walking alongside.

- **A young or inexperienced horse** should never be ridden on the road until it has proved itself in a controlled situation.

- **Riders should wear** high-visibility clothing to allow drivers the earliest chance of seeing them and driving with caution.

▲ *Even during the summer months when visibility is generally good, a rider wearing a fluorescent tabard helps drivers to see them, particularly when moving into areas of shade on an otherwise bright road.*

- **A riding hat that meets** current safety standards should always be worn, together with a body protector.

- **Observation is one of the keys** to road safety. The rider should keep away from busy main roads and be alert to moving traffic, continually looking and listening for hazards that may alarm the horse.

- **Riders should give** clear and accurate signals to inform other road users where they are going.

- **Parked vehicles** should be given sufficient berth to allow a passenger to open a door without injuring the horse or rider.

- **Riders should inform** someone of their planned route and the time it will take them to complete it, so an alarm can be raised if they fail to return.

▲ *Horse and rider should be well prepared and wear suitable equipment for travelling on the road.*

- **A mobile phone should be carried** in order to call for help in the event of an emergency. Phones should be switched to silent mode while riding to avoid startling the horse with a ringing tone.

Stabling

- **Stables are used** to shelter a horse from the extremes of weather.

- **An average-sized stable** is 3.7 x 3.7 m (12 x 12 ft).

- **A stable should be built** with its back to the prevailing wind on level ground with an area of hard standing to the front. If left as grass, this ground will quickly become churned up in wet weather.

- **The stable** and its doors should be of adequate height so the horse does not bang its head.

- **Stables must** have good ventilation to ensure the air inside does not become stale.

- **An overhang** at the front of the stable provides shade and protection from wind and rain.

- **The floor** of the stable should be non-slippery and hard-wearing. Concrete with rubber matting is often used as it can be washed down and disinfected easily.

▲ *The stable door should be high enough for the horse to easily walk through without banging its head. This door height is too low for the horse.*

- **Stable doors** are usually divided in two halves, so the top part can be fastened back and the stabled horse can see out and have access to fresh air. The doorway should be wide enough to allow the horse to pass through it comfortably. The top edge of the bottom door should be protected by a metal strip to stop the horse chewing it.

- **Stables should be** cleaned out regularly, and droppings and wet material removed daily.

- **Horses kept** in stables for long periods without any form of exercise can develop behavioural problems such as weaving, crib-biting, windsucking and box walking (see behavioural problems).

▲ *Horses are well-protected from rain and wind by the overhang on these stables. They also allow horses to see their companions.*

Common ailments

- **COPD** (chronic obstructive pulmonary disorder) is an allergy commonly caused by dust or mould spores. It affects a horse's breathing and may result in a cough or nasal discharge. The horse should be seen by a vet. It is usually recommended that the horse spends as much time in the fresh air as possible, its stable is kept clean and dust free, and its hay is soaked in water so any dust or mould spores swell in size and are less easily inhaled.

- **Thrush** affects the underside of the hoof around the frog. It is often caused by unhygienic bedding or standing in wet muddy conditions. It can be identified by its foul smell.

- **An abscess** on the sole of the foot can produce dramatic lameness in a horse. It is a common problem often caused by small puncture wounds that allow infection to enter the foot. The abscess is usually drained and poulticed to draw out any remaining infection.

- **Horses can go lame** for a variety of reasons and it is usually detected in one of two ways. If the horse is lame in a front leg, it will raise its head as the sore leg hits the ground. Lameness in hind legs is harder to establish, but will show in unevenness in a horse's hip when being trotted.

- Ear mites cause irritation – an affected horse might shake its head and try to scratch its ears. The condition can be treated with creams.

- **Aural plaques** are wart-like flakes in the ears and are usually harmless.

- **Colic is abdominal pain** – it can usually be detected if a horse is looking agitated and uncomfortable, kicking at its stomach and trying to roll. Swollen patches may also appear over its body. Veterinary advice and treatment is essential as it is a potentially fatal illness.

▶ *Mud fever affects a horse's heels and lower legs and shows as sore, reddened, scabbed skin.*

- **Lice live on horses,** causing bald patches as the horse tries to itch the affected areas, and can be transferred by grooming with another horse's brush. Louse powders and shampoos are used to treat the problem.

- **Mud fever** is usually caused by standing in wet and muddy fields. Bacteria enter the softened skin around the legs and needs to be treated with special anti-bacterial washes and creams.

- **Laminitis** is inflammation of the sensitive laminae in a horse's foot and is very painful. It is likely to occur if a pony grazes for too long on overly lush or fresh grass. A horse might lie down or stand with its weight on its heels in an attempt to ease the pain. The hooves will feel warm when touched and a vet needs to be called immediately.

Behavioural problems

- **Behavioural problems or vices** can be the result of stress or boredom. If a horse is confined in a stable alone over long periods of time, it will become unhappy and will often develop unwelcome habits. The solution is often to turn out the horse for longer periods and in the company of other horses.

- **Weaving** occurs when a horse stands at an open stable door repeatedly swinging its head from one side to another. Boxwalking is a pattern of behaviour where the horse refuses to settle and walks repeatedly around the confines of its stable.

- **Crib-biting** is the habit of biting or chewing wood. Considerable damage can be caused to gates, fencing and stables.

- **Windsucking** is similar to crib-biting – the horse attaches its teeth to a piece of wood and sucks in air.

- **If a horse starts to misbehave** when ridden, it may not be bad behaviour, especially if the behaviour is unusual, but a response to pain.

- **If a horse begins to buck**, particularly when asked to canter, the problem may lie with the saddle that should be checked immediately.

- **If a horse begins to headshake**, this may indicate a tooth problem and a professional horse dentist should examine its teeth.

- **If a horse shows reluctance** to be saddled, the saddle should be checked immediately. Massaging the back and stretching might be helpful, particularly for an older horse.

▲ *A rearing horse is dangerous for any rider. Immediate action should be taken to find and remove the cause.*

- **If after checking** the tack and consulting professionals the horse's behaviour is still poor or dangerous, it may require further schooling to ensure it understands and obeys basic aids.

- **The rider** may also benefit from further riding lessons to ensure aids are being given correctly and that they are not putting themselves in any danger from the horse.

Horse whispering

- **Horse whispering has moved** from folklore to established practice.

- **People now understand** and appreciate it is a means of communicating in the way a horse naturally understands.

- **Horses have a range** of ways of communicating with each other. This range spans vocalizing with neighs and whickers, minor visual signs, such as flicking an ear or clamping down a tail, to posturing, such as striking out with a leg or rearing, and body stances that can indicate submission or dominance.

- **By learning 'horse language'**, problems can be sorted out more effectively. By understanding that the horse is a flight animal who will run away from perceived danger the trainer can begin to work out how best to deal with the horse.

- **If a horse is approached** directly by a person who is square on and looking it directly in the eye, the horse will see this as someone who is confrontational, and may flee. The person should stand still, eyes averted, in a welcoming posture with a shoulder dipped in the direction of the horse. The horse might then feel able to approach. If it is not interested, the person can walk in large arcs backwards and forwards towards the horse and possibly be accepted.

- **Horses have basic signs** of submission, such as licking and chewing and dropping the head down low. A horse showing such signs does not want to go against the herd leader, which could be a human.

- **Horses move each other on** by walking behind another horse's flanks and possibly nudging them with their noses. A human can also move a horse in this way by walking behind and slightly to the side of the horse.

- **Horses have a natural fear** of many things. Humans cannot expect them not to be afraid but they can be trained not to run away, to trust their carer and accept that they will not be put in any real danger.

- **Many horse communicators** use special halters. These make it easier for the handler to teach the horse the difference between acceptable and unacceptable behaviour.

- **Monty Roberts is a leading** US exponent of horse whispering and has done much to establish it around the world.

▶ *Horses often form a strong relationship with another horse they live with – this is called pair-bonding. These horses have closer relationships with each other than with other horses in their field.*

Buying a horse

- **Horses and ponies** can be bought and sold in a variety of ways: by personal introduction, from a dealer, by advertisement and at auction.

- **Before purchase**, it is important to find out as much as possible about the horse's history and ability. It is also important to consider its age, size, temperament and conformation. A responsible seller should be able to produce a feeding programme and veterinary and worming records.

- **An animal's price** will vary according to its type, age, experience and quality. However, all horses and ponies should be vetted prior to purchase by an equine veterinary surgeon. During the vetting, the health and suitability will be examined and assessed.

▲ *A companion pony might be relatively cheap to buy, but will need the same standard of vet and farrier care as other horses.*

- **Blood tests and X-rays** can also be part of the vetting procedure.

- **Horses take time** to settle into new homes and may show untypical behaviour for the first weeks after a move, such as wood chewing or box walking, while they adapt to their new surroundings, horses and owner.

- **Horses require** twice-daily attention and year-round care. Anyone considering the purchase of a horse must be prepared and fully aware of the costs and time involved.

- **The purchase price** is only a small part of the cost of keeping the animal, which will include grazing, stabling, vetting, feeding, worming, tack and insurance.

- **Although many horses** can and will live alone, they are herd animals by nature and thrive on company. When buying a horse or pony, it is worth considering providing it with a companion. Horses that are no longer suitable for riding, either because of age or disability, will be advertised for sale on this basis.

- **Horses are sometimes sold** with tack. Always check it to ensure that it does not cause any problems, and that it is in a safe condition and does not need to be restitched or reflocked.

- **When it is time to sell** a horse it is important to ensure its owner can load it into a lorry or trailer without upset, so that the move is as gentle as possible. This may require several weeks' practice in advance.

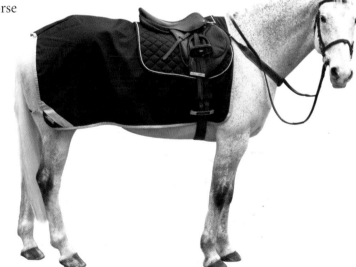

▶ *Before buying a horse determine whether the price includes tack and equipment.*

37

Welfare organizations

- **All domestic animals deserve** to be well-treated. Equine welfare organizations work towards protecting all horses, ponies and donkeys.

- **The International League** for the Protection of Horses (ILPH) was set up in England in 1927 by Ada Cole. The main aim was to 'prevent the ill-treatment of horses exported to Europe for slaughter'.

- **The ILPH organization** is now one of the world's leading equine welfare charities and works to help horseowners and relieve suffering in animals.

- **In Britain**, the ILPH has four rehabilitation and recovery centres caring for about 300 horses.

▲ *International and national charities and organizations work worldwide to protect the best interests of horses, donkeys and mules.*

- **In Britain**, as in the USA, there is legislation to protect horses. If someone is convicted of a serious offence against a horse they can be sent to prison and fined.

- **There are laws** that specifically relate to performing animals, and those that regulate accommodation, pasture and horses' health and welfare in riding schools.

- **Farriers are bound by laws** that aim to ensure horses are not subjected to unnecessary suffering by being shod by unskilled people.

- **The British Horse Society** is the UK's largest equine charity, aiming to improve the welfare of horses and ponies and promote the interests of its member horseowners and riders.

- **The Donkey Sanctuary** in England was set up 30 years ago by Dr Elisabeth Svendsen and has cared for almost 9000 donkeys.

- **The International Donkey Protection Trust** was also established by Dr Svendsen and works worldwide to improve conditions for working donkeys and mules in Europe, Africa, Egypt, India and Mexico.

▲ *Ponies living wild need to be monitored to make sure they are healthy. Welfare charities offer support and advice for owners and can take action if animals are in poor condition.*

39

Index

40